Monthly Bill ORGANIZER and Planner Notebook

Creative Bill Organizers and Planners

MONTH *of* YEAR

PAYABLE TO	AMOUNT	DUE ON	PAID

MONTH *of* ______ YEAR ______

PAYABLE TO	AMOUNT	DUE ON	PAID

MONTH *of* YEAR

PAYABLE TO	AMOUNT	DUE ON	PAID

MONTH *of* ______ YEAR ______

PAYABLE TO	AMOUNT	DUE ON	PAID

Month:

Monday	Tuesday	Wednesday	Thursday

Friday	Saturday	Sunday	

Month:

Monday	Tuesday	Wednesday	Thursday

Friday	Saturday	Sunday	

Month:

Monday	Tuesday	Wednesday	Thursday

Friday	Saturday	Sunday	

Month:

Monday	Tuesday	Wednesday	Thursday

Friday	Saturday	Sunday

MONTH *of* YEAR

PAYABLE TO	AMOUNT	DUE ON	PAID

MONTH *of* ______ YEAR ______

PAYABLE TO	AMOUNT	DUE ON	PAID

MONTH *of* ______ YEAR ______

PAYABLE TO	AMOUNT	DUE ON	PAID

MONTH *of* ______ YEAR ______

PAYABLE TO	AMOUNT	DUE ON	PAID

Month:

Monday	Tuesday	Wednesday	Thursday

Friday	Saturday	Sunday	

Month:

Monday	Tuesday	Wednesday	Thursday

Friday	Saturday	Sunday	

Month:

Monday	Tuesday	Wednesday	Thursday

Friday	Saturday	Sunday	

Month:

Monday	Tuesday	Wednesday	Thursday

Friday	Saturday	Sunday	

MONTH *of* YEAR

PAYABLE TO	AMOUNT	DUE ON	PAID

MONTH *of* YEAR

PAYABLE TO	AMOUNT	DUE ON	PAID

MONTH *of* ______ YEAR ______

PAYABLE TO	AMOUNT	DUE ON	PAID

MONTH *of* ______ YEAR ______

PAYABLE TO	AMOUNT	DUE ON	PAID

Month:

Monday	Tuesday	Wednesday	Thursday

Friday	Saturday	Sunday	

Month:

Monday	Tuesday	Wednesday	Thursday

Friday	Saturday	Sunday	

Month:

Monday	Tuesday	Wednesday	Thursday

Friday	Saturday	Sunday	

Month:

Monday	Tuesday	Wednesday	Thursday

Friday	Saturday	Sunday	

MONTH *of* ______ YEAR ______

PAYABLE TO	AMOUNT	DUE ON	PAID

MONTH *of* ______ YEAR ______

PAYABLE TO	AMOUNT	DUE ON	PAID

MONTH *of* ______ YEAR ______

PAYABLE TO	AMOUNT	DUE ON	PAID

MONTH *of* ____________ YEAR ____________

PAYABLE TO	AMOUNT	DUE ON	PAID

Month:

Monday	Tuesday	Wednesday	Thursday

Friday	Saturday	Sunday	

Month:

Monday	Tuesday	Wednesday	Thursday

Friday	Saturday	Sunday	

Month:

Monday	Tuesday	Wednesday	Thursday

Friday	Saturday	Sunday	

Month:

Monday	Tuesday	Wednesday	Thursday

Friday	Saturday	Sunday	

MONTH *of* ________ YEAR ________

PAYABLE TO	AMOUNT	DUE ON	PAID

MONTH *of* YEAR

PAYABLE TO	AMOUNT	DUE ON	PAID

MONTH *of* YEAR

PAYABLE TO	AMOUNT	DUE ON	PAID

MONTH *of* ____________ YEAR ____________

PAYABLE TO	AMOUNT	DUE ON	PAID

Month:

Monday	Tuesday	Wednesday	Thursday

Friday	Saturday	Sunday	

Month:

Monday	Tuesday	Wednesday	Thursday

Friday	Saturday	Sunday	

Month:

Monday	Tuesday	Wednesday	Thursday

Friday	Saturday	Sunday	

Month:

Monday	Tuesday	Wednesday	Thursday

Friday	Saturday	Sunday

MONTH *of* ______ YEAR ______

PAYABLE TO	AMOUNT	DUE ON	PAID

MONTH *of* YEAR

PAYABLE TO	AMOUNT	DUE ON	PAID

MONTH *of* ______ YEAR ______

PAYABLE TO	AMOUNT	DUE ON	PAID

MONTH *of* YEAR

PAYABLE TO	AMOUNT	DUE ON	PAID

Month:

Monday	Tuesday	Wednesday	Thursday

Friday	Saturday	Sunday	

Month:

Monday	Tuesday	Wednesday	Thursday

Friday	Saturday	Sunday	

Month:

Monday	Tuesday	Wednesday	Thursday

Friday	Saturday	Sunday	

Month:

Monday	Tuesday	Wednesday	Thursday

Friday	Saturday	Sunday	

Topic of the Day: ______

Today's Date: ______

Topic of the Day: ______________________________

Today's Date: ______________________________

Topic of the Day: ____________________

Today's Date: ____________________

Topic of the Day:

Today's Date:

Topic of the Day:

Today's Date:

Topic of the Day:

Today's Date:

Topic of the Day: ______________________________

Today's Date: ______________________________

Topic of the Day:

Today's Date:

Topic of the Day:

Today's Date:

Topic of the Day: ________________

Today's Date: ________________

Topic of the Day: ____________________

Today's Date: ____________________

Topic of the Day:

Today's Date:

Topic of the Day:

Today's Date:

Topic of the Day:

Today's Date:

Topic of the Day:

Today's Date:

Topic of the Day:

Today's Date:

Topic of the Day:

Today's Date:

Topic of the Day: ______________________________

Today's Date: ______________________________

Topic of the Day:

Today's Date:

Topic of the Day:

Today's Date:

Topic of the Day:

Today's Date:

Topic of the Day:

Today's Date:

Topic of the Day: ______________________________

Today's Date: ______________________________

Topic of the Day:

Today's Date:

Topic of the Day: ____________________

Today's Date: ____________________

Topic of the Day:

Today's Date:

Topic of the Day:

Today's Date:

Topic of the Day:

Today's Date:

Topic of the Day: ____________________

Today's Date: ____________________

Topic of the Day: ____________________

Today's Date: ____________________

Topic of the Day: ______________________

Today's Date: ______________________

Topic of the Day:

Today's Date:

Topic of the Day:

Today's Date:

Topic of the Day:

Today's Date:

Topic of the Day: ______

Today's Date: ______

Topic of the Day:

Today's Date:

Topic of the Day:

Today's Date:

Topic of the Day: ______________________

Today's Date: ______________________

Topic of the Day:

Today's Date:

Topic of the Day:

Today's Date:

Topic of the Day: ____________________

Today's Date: ____________________

Topic of the Day: ____________________

Today's Date: ____________________

Topic of the Day: ________________________

Today's Date: ________________________

Topic of the Day: ______________________

Today's Date: ______________________

Topic of the Day: ____________________

Today's Date: ____________________

Topic of the Day:

Today's Date:

Topic of the Day: ______________________

Today's Date: ______________________

Topic of the Day:

Today's Date:

Topic of the Day: ____________________

Today's Date: ____________________

Topic of the Day:

Today's Date:

Topic of the Day: ______

Today's Date: ______

Topic of the Day: ______________________________

Today's Date: ______________________________

Topic of the Day:

Today's Date:

Topic of the Day:

Today's Date:

Topic of the Day:

Today's Date:

Topic of the Day:

Today's Date:

Topic of the Day: ____________________

Today's Date: ____________________

Topic of the Day:

Today's Date:

Topic of the Day:

Today's Date:

Topic of the Day: ______________________________

Today's Date: ______________________________

Topic of the Day:

Today's Date:

Topic of the Day:

Today's Date:

Topic of the Day:

Today's Date:

Topic of the Day:

Today's Date:

Topic of the Day:

Today's Date:

Topic of the Day: ______________________

Today's Date: ______________________

Topic of the Day: ______

Today's Date: ______

Topic of the Day:

Today's Date:

Topic of the Day:

Today's Date:

Topic of the Day:

Today's Date:

Topic of the Day: ____________________

Today's Date: ____________________

Topic of the Day:

Today's Date:

Topic of the Day: ______________________

Today's Date: ______________________

Topic of the Day: ______________________

Today's Date: ______________________

Topic of the Day: ______________________________

Today's Date: ______________________________

Topic of the Day:

Today's Date:

Topic of the Day: ______________________________

Today's Date: ______________________________

Topic of the Day:

Today's Date:

Topic of the Day:

Today's Date:

Topic of the Day:

Today's Date:

Topic of the Day:

Today's Date:

Topic of the Day:

Today's Date:

Topic of the Day:

Today's Date:

Topic of the Day: ____________________

Today's Date: ____________________

Made in United States
North Haven, CT
02 October 2023

42270009R00089